Prayers and Meditations of Susanna Wesley

Edited by
Dr Michael D McMullen

Front Cover photograph courtesy of Judges Postcards Ltd, Hastings

© 2000 Trustees for Methodist Church Purposes

ISBN 1 85852 150 5

CONTENTS

Foreword   1

Prayers of

Personal Devotion   5

Christian Living   14

Personal Holiness   32

Repentance   38

Prayers in Times of

Joy and Thanksgiving   47

Trouble or Difficulty   57

Temptation   63

Meditations on

The Nature of God   73

The Blessings of God   85

The Lord's Day   95

Notes and Sources   103

Subject Index   107

This book is dedicated to all the members and friends of my first Pastorate, the Harestanes Congregation of Kirkintilloch Baptist Church, Scotland. But I would like to make this a special dedication to the memory of those saints who went to be with the Lord during my time of ministry there:

Isa Crawford
Catherine Greenshields
Susan Hoey
Maisie McBrearty
Nettie Sim
Bessie Smith
Colin Smith

Foreword

Susanna Wesley (1669-1742) was heir to a rich blend of Christian traditions. She was the daughter of Dr Samuel Annesley, one of the leading Puritan ministers in seventeenth-century London. She was therefore reared in Dissent, but at the age of thirteen, having studied the issues between the Church and the Nonconformists, she decided to join the Church of England, from which her father had been excluded in 1662. To his great credit, Dr Annesley fully accepted her conscientious decision and looked upon her as his favourite daughter to the end of his life.

Susanna's *Prayers and Meditations* reflect this twofold religious inheritance. They breathe a sober, reasoned Anglican piety, strongly moralistic and concerned to love God with the whole mind. They also make clear that Susanna remained true to the Puritan spirituality in which she was raised, with its concern for 'serious godliness' and personal experience. Her meditation which begins, 'When I examine myself three times a day . . .', refers to her 'method' of devotion, which led her to set aside an hour morning and evening, with a briefer break at noon, for private daily prayer and meditation. Her aim was 'to employ my thoughts and time in a strict conscientious performance of present duty' ('Lord, I love you', p 31). Yet if her piety was strict and conscientious, it was also filled with joy and thankfulness, as her prayers reveal. She is grateful for all mercies, small and great. She shows her ardent love of God and her joy in doing his will, so that in the meditation just cited she concludes with a spontaneous outburst of praise: 'Glory be to you, O Lord.'

Susanna's regular cycle of prayer challenges comparison with the ordered devotion of a religious community, and it has indeed been compared to the life of the cloister, carried on in the lonely parsonage in the Lincolnshire Fens, where her husband was Rector of Epworth. Yet what makes Susanna's version of the contemplative life so heroic is that it was maintained in the midst of the extraordinarily demanding life of the mother of a large family. She bore Samuel, who was by no means easy to live with, nineteen children, ten of whom survived infancy. The family often felt the pinch of poverty, and Susanna was dogged by ill-health, not surprisingly in view of the constant strain of child-bearing. Yet with all these trials to contend with, she devoted herself to the education – spiritual, moral and general – of her children. She set up her own little school in the Rectory and taught them for six hours a day.

1

The cares and troubles of her life understandably find their way into her meditations, as she strives constantly to perceive and do God's holy and blessed will. So, for example, in 'The Way to the Father' (p 69), she breaks out into the heartfelt cry:

> O my God,
> if it will please you indeed to bless me,
> and deliver me from temptations,
> if you will vouchsafe to give me food to eat
> and raiment to put on,
> without debt;
> without this extreme distress;
> then I will offer up my self absolutely,
> entirely to Jesus Christ,
> the Incarnate God,
> the only Saviour of the world!

Susanna was a highly-educated, well-read woman, with a keen theological mind. She might well have become embittered and frustrated by the constraints of her narrow material circumstances at Epworth. Instead, she sought to find God's will and fulfil her Christian vocation precisely where she was placed. She concentrates all her prayer, her mind and heart, her gifts and talents, on her calling as a Christian wife and mother. Devoting herself utterly to her children, she is content to fill a little space, if God be glorified. Today, of course, a woman with Susanna's gifts would probably be teaching theology in a university or fulfilling some other role as a professional educationist. In seventeenth-century England, that was impossible for her. Instead, she vows, single-mindedly, 'I must . . . do what good I can, especially to the souls God has committed to my care' ('Seize the Opportunity', p7). 'Purity of heart,' says Kierkegaard, 'is to will one thing.' The fruit of Susanna's willing that one thing is to be seen in the lives of her sons, Samuel, John and Charles, and her seven lively and intelligent daughters.

Dr Michael McMullen has edited, with great care and clarity, Susanna's *Prayers and Meditations*. In doing so, he has provided a rich source for contemporary spiritual reading, and he has allowed us to glimpse the greatness of the woman who has been fairly described as 'The Mother of Methodism'.

Rev Dr John A Newton
Warden of John Wesley's Chapel
(The New Room) Bristol

PRAYERS OF

PERSONAL DEVOTION
CHRISTIAN LIVING
PERSONAL HOLINESS
REPENTANCE

TRUE FRIENDSHIP

Enable me to live so as to deserve a friend,
and if I never have one on earth,
you be my friend,
for in having you
I shall have all that is dear and valuable in friendship.

Though a good name is as precious ointment,
yet I remember
that I have offered up mine to you, my God,
and have resolved never to make my reputation
or the esteem of man
the end of any of my actions,
where your glory is not concerned.

TRUE RICHES

I know that this world is but for a short time.
Oh, that our treasure and hearts might be in heaven;
For it is then that we would not need to be,
nor would we be,
very solicitous about temporal concerns.

Help me to regard honour, riches,
and sensual pleasures as they are,
namely vain, unsatisfactory, perishing trifles;
not worth much care to get or keep.

We will not barter heaven and eternal happiness
for things which,
in themselves considered,
have no real value.
In fact,
help us see that they are rather a clog and burden
to souls that are truly devoted to you.

We would rather enjoy the blessed opportunities
of frequent retirement from the world,
than possess all those things
which foolish, mistaken men
account the chief ingredients of happiness.

For we know that we were born to die;
and we are assured
that this life is but a prelude to eternity,
and this short, uncertain space of time
is all that is allowed for the working out of our salvation.

We know, too, that wealth, honour and fame
which, even if it is obtained,
can neither satisfy in the enjoyment,
nor be kept one moment after death.

SEIZE THE OPPORTUNITY

When I examine myself three times a day,
help me to do it more accurately;
let no trifling matter divert me,
for though it takes not much time,
it is certain that opportunities once lost
can never be recovered.

May it be that whatever my hand finds to do,
I will do with all my might.
When I have an opportunity, therefore,
I will thankfully and vigorously make use of it,
remembering that for all these things
God will bring me to judgement.

Saviour,
I remember that when on earth
you went about doing good.
I must also do what good I can,
especially to the souls God has committed to my care,
and help me not to be discouraged by infirmities or work.

REDEEM THE TIME

Lord, I would begin and end the day with you –
the Alpha and Omega –
and if I really experience what it is to love you,
then I will redeem all the time I can
for your immediate service.

For I remember the rule I lived under
when in my father's house,
when I had as little – if not less – liberty than I have now.
I used to allow myself as much time for recreation
as I spent in private devotion;
not that I always spent so much,
but I gave myself leave to go so far but no farther.

THE NAME OF THE LORD

I will fall down and kneel before the Lord my Maker.
And in all my external actions,
I will seek to observe a due composure and decency,
as becomes one that takes upon herself
the honour to approach near
and speak unto so great a Majesty!

As I assent to your being,
your unity and your perfections,
and as I seek to worship you
in a manner agreeable to your nature –
in spirit and in truth,
so help me likewise,
to truly honour your Name.

And remind me to be always very careful
to speak nothing but the truth,
out of a high esteem and veneration for your Name,
by which it has pleased
the Most High God to make himself known
to the children of men.

And in all places,
and at all times,
whenever I have occasion to make use of your sacred Name,
I will do it with an awful regard to your presence,
with great humility and the profoundest reverence,
especially when I speak
to the great and glorious God.

A LIVING SACRIFICE

What shall I render to you for all your mercies?
The little unworthy praise that I can offer
is so mean and contemptible an offering,
that I am even ashamed to tender it.
But, Lord, accept it for the sake of Christ
and pardon the deficiencies of the sacrifice.

I would if I dared,
humbly offer you my self and all that you have given me,
and I would resolve –
Oh, give me grace to do it –
that the residue of my life
shall all be devoted to your service.

And I do intend
to be more particularly careful of the soul of this child,
that you have so mercifully provided for,
than ever I have been,
that I may do my endeavour to instil into his mind
the principles of your true religion and virtue.
Lord, give me grace to do it sincerely and prudently,
and bless my attempts with good success.

LIVING IN GOD'S PRESENCE

Almighty God,
you are the One my reason declares
to be the Author of my being,
and the One from whom
I derive all things necessary for my support.

Enable me, therefore,
to practise an unfeigned subjection of myself towards you.
Save me
from the want of consideration and advertence
to these first principles of religion.

May I be careful,
to maintain a constant, habitual sense of you in my mind;
to live and act as in your presence;
to think often of your power, wisdom, goodness, justice, truth
and above all,
of your infinite purity,
that it may be a check upon my mind
and the best preservative against all temptations.

OBEDIENCE IS BETTER THAN SACRIFICE

My God and Father,
though I am often interrupted by bodily infirmities,
grant me patience and submission,
remembering that obedience is better than sacrifice.

I thank you for my being and preservation,
for my food and raiment,
but chiefly for what is infinitely more than all we can receive
of temporal blessings,
in that you have sent your only Son into the world
to save sinners,
and for this one infinite and inestimable mercy
I would praise and adore you to all eternity.

TRUST IN THE LORD

O God,
I thank you for the peculiar joy
which comes with peace of conscience
and for the pleasure and satisfaction of soul
when it is strengthened by your grace
to perform the several duties of life.

Help me in the extraordinary occurrences of life,
to keep my mind from being too warm
and from speaking too eagerly.
I trust you with all events
and beg your blessing upon my honest endeavours.
Help me to guard my mind this day
and inspire me with devotion in singing your praise.

PRACTISING THE PRESENCE OF GOD

Help me, Lord,
to remember that religion
is not to be confined to the church or closet,
nor exercised only in prayer and meditation,
but that everywhere I am in your presence.
So may my every word and action have a moral content.

HELP ME TO KNOW MYSELF

O Lord,
as defects and infirmities betray themselves
in the daily accidents
and common conversations of life,
grant me your grace,
that I may watch over, regulate and govern them.

Enable me
so to know myself and those with whom I have to do,
that I may conform to the precepts of the Gospel
and train myself
to those rules of wisdom and virtue of which I am capable.

Help me
to discern the proper season
and the just occasion of every virtue,
and then to apply myself to attain it,
by exercising it in those beneficent activities which,
for want of due reflection,
may not seem of any great importance.

PURIFY MY MIND

I would have my wealth to be your favour,
with all the blessed consequences attending it;
the virtues of your Holy Spirit,
purifying my mind,
exalting my nature to the dignity of a Divine resemblance,
teaching me
to undervalue whatever a mistaken world calls good,
as unnecessary or a hindrance
to that spiritual and eternal good
which I would prize above all others.

So I trust you
with the conduct of my soul,
committing myself to you in ways of well-doing,
praying that you will not suffer me
to do anything that would reasonably reflect
upon my Christian profession,
but enable me
to contemn the reputation of any quality or virtue
that terminates in myself.
Help me, O Lord, to do well.

TRUE CONTENTMENT

O God,
I have found that my peace and happiness
depend much on my own opinion of myself
and not that of others.
It is the inward sentiments I have of myself
that raise or deject me;
and my mind can no more be pleased
with any sensation but its own
than the body can be gratified by the relishes of another palate.

Save me from leading an imaginary life in the ideas of others,
and so to be eager and forward
in showing myself to the world.

Forbid that I should retain, improve and adorn
this fictitious being, while stupidly neglecting the true.
Help me not to contend with men's interests;
their prejudices and passions,
that rarely admit of a calm dispute,
when it can innocently be avoided.

May I be so far a lover of myself
as to prefer the peace and tranquillity of my own mind
before that of others,
and if after doing all that I can to make others happy,
they yet remain obstinately bent
to follow those ways that lead to misery,
I leave them to your mercy.

A GOOD CONSCIENCE

Lord, I resolve to keep
a conscience void of offence towards you and man,
for I see how many nowadays
seek to advance their worldly interest;
endeavour to raise their families by fraud and oppression;
and who make shipwreck of their faith and good consciences.

Let it, then, be my great care
to have a special regard to justice and charity;
to preserve the principles of faith inviolate;
and in all cases
to perform present duty
with the greatest exactness and integrity.

For I know
that whenever crosses or troubles are met without,
because of you, Lord,
all will be well within.

STRONG IN THE LORD

Our Lord,
give us strength
that we might not be weak,
that we might not in vanity speak of ourselves;
our families;
business;
relations and acquaintances.

Help us to see that the opinion of man
is of so little consequence,
since it possibly may no way
conduce to our eternal happiness,
nor will it add any weight to our eternal glory.

Help us to see that it is he who walks uprightly
who walks most securely.
That even if we incur the displeasure of men,
we are always assured of your favour and protection.
That you can, if you see it best for us,
can make our righteousness –
shine as the sun;
and our just dealing –
appear as the noon-day.

FAMILY RESPONSIBILITIES

I know, Lord,
that though the care and education of so many children
must create abundance of trouble,
and will perpetually keep the mind employed –
as well as the body;
yet I will consider it no small honour
to be entrusted with the care of so many souls.
For I know too, Lord,
that if that trust be but managed with prudence and integrity,
the harvest will abundantly recompense the toil of the seed-time.

Help me to know, too,
that it will be certainly no little accession to the future glory
to stand forth at the last day and say,
'Lord, here are the children which you have given me,
of whom I have lost none
by my ill example;
nor by my neglecting to instil into their minds,
in their early years,
the principles of your true religion and virtue.'

LOVE NOT THE WORLD

Lord,
by your Apostle John you have told us,
love not the world,
nor the things that are in the world,
for it is the heart that you require.

Enable me to fix my affections not on sensual pleasures,
riches, or honours,
for if I allow my heart – my affections –
to centre on anything but you,
I actually make that thing my god,
and in so doing forfeit my title and pretensions
to eternal happiness.

THE VIRTUE OF OBEDIENCE

Blessed God,
because the Christian religion is so complicated in its nature,
help me to give myself entirely to its discipline,
that I might steadfastly adhere to its precepts.
Enable me to practise those virtues
that mutually assist and strengthen each other:
thus temperance and chastity;
fortitude and truth;
humility and patience; and
Divine charity and charity towards man.

And because all virtues are closely bound together,
help me not to break but one link of the golden chain,
so that I will not spoil the whole contexture.

THE MOST POWERFUL TEACHER

Lord,
my mind is naturally so corrupted
and all the powers thereof so weakened
that I cannot possibly aspire vigorously towards you,
or have any clear perception of spiritual things
without your assistance.

Therefore, nothing less than the same Almighty power
that raised Jesus Christ from the dead
can raise my soul from the death of sin to a life of holiness.
That is why to know you experimentally
is altogether supernatural
and something I could never attain to
but by the merits and intercession of Jesus Christ.

By virtue of what you have done and suffered
and are now doing in heaven for me,
You give us your Holy Spirit,
who is the best Instructor
and the most powerful Teacher I can possibly have,
and without whose agency
all other means of grace would be ineffectual.

How certainly does he assist and strengthen my soul,
if it is sincere and hearty in its endeavours
to avoid any evil or to perform any good!
May he enable me to have a good desire
and a fervent aspiration toward you my God,
longings that shall not pass unregarded.

ONLY GOD CAN SATISFY

You only, O God,
can satisfy my immortal soul
and bestow on me those spiritual pleasures,
which alone are proper to its nature.
Grant me grace to stay and centre my soul in you,
that its desires, hopes and expectations of happiness
might be confined only to you;
and that I might have a firm, habitual resignation to your will.

Oh, that I might love you, my God,
with all my heart,
with all my mind,
and with all my strength!
That I might so love you as I desire you;
that I might so desire you as to be uneasy without you –
without your favour,
without some such resemblance to you
as my nature in this imperfect state can bear.

SAVED BY GRACE

Forbid it, Lord,
that I should entertain too high a conceit of myself,
especially when moving amongst people
who are licentious in their lives
and observe no rule in their actions,
lest I should proclaim a superior holiness,
so turning your grace into wantonness
and forgetting that it is you who has made me so to differ.
To whom be glory!

KNOWING GOD

You have taught me, Lord,
that to pursue after knowledge only for its own sake,
is a vain and unprofitable curiosity.
To labour for it only that I may be applauded by others,
is still worse,
and displays a vain-glorious, weak and childish temper.

Such knowledge puffs up
and is directly opposite to divine charity –
the love of God –
which alone edifies,
or establishes the soul in all Christian virtues.

We must know that we may love,
we must love that we may cheerfully obey,
and we must obey,
that we may please God.

Knowledge that goes no farther than speculation,
is like an excellent instrument
in the hand of an unskilled person
who knows not how to make use of it.

The wisdom I earnestly pray for,
is that wisdom that goes on to practise
the general rules it has understood.

MAN'S FIRST DUTY

Almighty God,
the Great Father of Spirits,
you made us yourself;
and you know perfectly the works of your own omnipotence.
You know the powers of our minds,
their various motions and springs of action.

You have required that the first instance
of our duty toward you must be
that we love the Lord our God
with all the heart,
with all the mind,
with all the soul,
and with all the strength that we have.

GOD ANSWERS PRAYER

God is Truth,
and it is obviously impossible
that your Word should ever fail.
You never said to any of your creatures:
'Seek ye my face or favour' in vain.
And again you said:
'Ask and ye shall receive,
seek and ye shall find,
knock and it shall be opened unto you.'

Why is it then that my prayers are not answered?
It cannot be that you are unmindful
or unwilling or unable to grant my petitions.
Why then should it be?
I am asking from myself and I receive not,
because I ask amiss.

I either ask irreverently,
which is rather a demanding than a begging grace,
which argues want of reverence and humility;
or I ask coldly without being appraised
of the value of that grace that I pray for,
and so I do not in good earnest desire it.
It is no wonder I see no answer.

Perhaps my desires spring,
not from a principle of love to God
and a high estimation of holiness,
nor from a zeal for your glory
and a hearty desire to be conformed to your image and will,
but it may be I ask for grace
that I may be assured of your protection in this world.

Perhaps I ask that I may enjoy a greater affluence
of temporal blessings;
or that I may be applauded and esteemed by man;

and can one really believe that God
will prostitute his noblest gifts to such an unworthy creature?

You are a great and a jealous God,
nor will you admit a rival in your love;
nor impart grace and favour
to such as would divide their affections
between him and the world.
We must give you all our heart,
or you will accept of none of it.

You require that such as take upon themselves
the honour of speaking to you,
should approach you with the most profound humility;
with the highest reverence and devotion;
with a heart separated from the world;
devoted to your glory;
and that we most highly esteem,
value and prize the grace which we petition for.

For what greater affront can we offer your Divine Majesty
than to ask with seeming devotion any virtue or grace
when we do not have the least regard whether we have it or not?

But suppose we offer our petitions to the Divine Majesty,
with the most profound reverence;
with humility;
with an earnest desire of those things we pray for;
and with an ardent zeal for the manifestations of his glory,
yet perhaps we ask impatiently,
we would indeed have grace,
but we would have it just then,
we are not willing to tarry the Lord's leisure.

Nor are willing to be at the pains of repeating our petitions,
and therefore if we are delayed,
though not denied,
our mind, instead of being more strongly united
to God by faith and love,

grows displeased and angry;
we say:

> 'What a weariness is it to serve the Lord?
> Or what profit is it that we serve the Almighty?'

Whether these or any other reason
prevents the answering of prayers,
this we may be assured of,
that God is infinite truth,
and since he has graciously promised to hear the prayers
that are made to him in the name of Christ,
he will certainly do it.

LORD, I LOVE YOU

How hard do I find it to be upon the guard,
to maintain a constant watch,
and a regular habitual advertence to my thought,
words and actions.
And it is this irregularity of temper and life
that interrupts the comforts which might be found in religion,
and renders my perseverance suspicious.

But this is my infirmity.
I ought to consider that God is always the same, fixed,
    immutable,
ever ready to succour and strengthen them
that truly and sincerely devote themselves to his service.

The whole tenor of the Gospel
insists upon sincerity as the main condition of salvation.
A sincere faith and obedience,
though the one may be weak and the other imperfect,
yet if they do but determine a person
to an habitual temper of obedience;
if they do but in the main prove a person devoted to God;
and that though they cannot with St Peter
appeal to that Omniscient Being that they do love him,
yet if they can but heartily say:
'Lord, you that know all things,
know that I desire nothing more than to love you.'

Surely God will make great allowances for infirmities,
temptations, sudden and unforeseen accidents,
nor ought I so frequently to admit of nice scruples,
and perplexing thoughts,
but rather employ my thoughts and time in a strict,
conscientious performance of present duty,
and so entirely depend on the infinite goodness of God
to secure me from future temptations.
Glory be to you, O Lord.

GROWING TOWARD GOD'S LIKENESS

May all happenings of my life
prove useful and beneficial to me.
May all things instruct me
and afford me an opportunity
of exercising some virtue and daily learning
and growing toward your likeness,
let the world go which way it will.

FOR MY CHILDREN

Oh, that it would please you, Almighty God,
to grant me this one petition,
that instead of making my children remarkable
for beauty, wit, riches, or honours,
the love of this your day might be engraved on their minds
in such indelible characters,
that they might by their deportment on the Lord's day,
be distinguished from the rest of the world.

Amen. Amen.

PURE SERVICE

Do we not yet know that God is a holy and a jealous God?
That he abhors all profane mixture
and worldly regards in his service?
How long will it be before we consider
and attain to that purity,
that perfect abstraction from all earthly things
that is required in such as take upon themselves
the honour of preaching the Divine Majesty?

TRUE DEVOTION

It is now about nine years
since I more solemnly devoted myself to your service,
and since I resolved to spend at least one hour
morning and evening in private duties,
which resolution I have adhered to,
and though by sickness
and sometimes unavoidable business
I have contracted my devotions,
yet not even my enemy can accuse me
of having once willingly omitted or shortened my private duties,
but I have and still do
usually so much exceed the allotted time.
Glory be to you, O Lord.

LORD OF CREATION

As you, Almighty God,
are the Creator of all beings
and by your sole power
you commanded the whole universe
to spring from nothing into being,
you must necessarily be the absolute Sovereign
and Proprietor of whatever you have created.

Your dominion,
your jurisdiction is founded on the act of creation
and you have an authority over us as creatures,
before you have dominion over us as converts.

And as this is a strong foundation
for a claim of authority over man,
so it lays the strong obligation on man
to be in entire subjection to you.
Shall not all creatures
that received their very being from you,
and that entirely depend on you,
be subject unto you?

You are, O Lord,
the only God for whom all things were created.
The Supreme God
must necessarily act for the best and noblest end.
Nor can we conceive any end in working worthy of you,
but your own glory,
which we see displayed
in all your works of Creation and Providence.

And, therefore, since you have made all things for yourself,
and since you only preserve what you have made,
and each individual of the Creation entirely depends on you
for all they do or can enjoy,
it is but just and reasonable
that they acknowledge their dependence,
and that you have created them,
and that they receive their blessings
from your bounty and goodness which is glorifying you.

WATCH AND PRAY

You have called us, O Lord,
to watch and pray.
Therefore, whatever may be the sin against which I pray,
make me careful to watch against it,
and so have reason to expect
that my prayer will be answered.

In order to perform this duty aright,
grant me:
grace to preserve a sober, equal temper;
sincerity to pray for your assistance;
remembering also that sobriety and equality of mind
consist in freedom from all perturbation.

RESTING AND TRUSTING

Help me, O God,
to fortify my mind with patience,
submission and renewed repentance,
that I may be assured of Divine succours
when I most need them.

May I learn by practice
to love you above all things,
that so I may be out of the power of the world
and my earthly circumstances give me no uneasiness.

THE LORD'S SUPPER

O Lord,
that we might always prepare ourselves
when we come to the Lord's Supper.

That we would examine ourselves
whether we
truly repent of our former sins;
steadfastly purpose to lead new lives;
have a lively faith in God's mercy through Christ,
with a thankful remembrance of his death;
and be in charity with all men.

GOD'S MERCY

O Lord, when I think of your holiness,
I fear that my repentance is partial
and that I have not remembered
the thousandth part of my transgressions.

Yet I know
that repentance and confession of themselves
have no merit in them.
It is only on the merits of Christ that I rely
for pardon and acceptance.

I renounce my own righteousness,
my own performances,
and rely only
on Jesus the Mediator of the New Covenant.
I humbly throw myself upon the mercy of God,
and beg that his grace may be actually sufficient for me –
that I might have a lively faith in God's mercy through Christ.

LORD OF ALL

Lord,
you are the only Disposer of events,
the Eternal, ever-blessèd God.
You created all things by your almighty power,
and you do whatever pleases you –
among the inhabitants of the earth,
as well as in the armies of heaven.

Therefore,
I would solemnly set apart some portion of time
to beg your more especial direction and assistance
upon that business
on which a great part of my future prosperity may depend.

I would in the first place,
humbly acknowledge and bewail all the errors
of my past life:
those that I can remember,
as well as those that have escaped my memory;
and I pray – as David did –
that you would cleanse me from my secret faults.

I would proceed then,
to praise you for all the mercies I have received
from your divine goodness.
I would then go on to beg your favour in this great affair –
and I would do all this in the Name
and through the mediation of
my blessèd Jesus.

CLEANSE ME, O LORD

Cleanse me, O Lord,
from my secret faults,
and keep me from presumptuous sins,
lest they get the dominion over me.

Remind me, Lord,
when I would attempt the conversion of others
that I must be careful in the first place
to reform myself.
And if I do not abstain myself
from gross and scandalous vices
I am of all others
the most unfit for a reformer.

God, the Great Lord of heaven and earth,
the Almighty Father of Spirits,
has placed all mankind in this world in a state of probation,
and has committed to each individual a stock of talents,
to some more, to some less,
commanding us to improve them for his glory.
Help me, therefore,
to look upon every child
as a talent committed to my trust.

And may I be assured that I must give an account
at the last great day
how I have discharged this trust,
and if through my default any soul miscarry,
how will I hold up my face in the last judgement?

ABUNDANT CLEANSING

Great and holy God,
I have much need of humbling myself before you,
because of the sins that I am daily guilty of:
in thought, word and deed,
against your Divine Majesty.

Help me, Lord,
to overcome habitual levity in my thoughts
and to shun vain and impure thoughts which,
though they do not take up their abode in my mind
for any length of time,
yet in their passing through,
often leave a tincture of impurity.

Enable me to watch over my heart, thoughts and affections
with all diligence,
for out of them are the issues of life.
How often have I offended in this way!
Cleanse me, Lord,
from my secret faults,
for out of the abundance of the heart the mouth speaks.

Help me, my God,
to guard against vain and unnecessary words,
and to speak of you with that reverence,
that humility, that gravity that I ought.

YOUR GRACE MAKES ME WHAT I AM

I praise you, O God,
for any ability to serve you
and for enabling me to perform relative duties,
which are a great part of natural and revealed religion.

I am apt to be discouraged
by the constant sense of my infirmities,
but you, O God,
will not despise the day of small things.
It is your grace that makes me what I am,
that keeps me to stated times of devotion
and that in any measure preserves me from total apostasy.

I know that my performances are mean and contemptible
and unworthy of your acceptance,
yet if you did not utterly reject them,
you would not so often give me grace to repent
and enable me to rejoice in any little victory which I get
over my daily infirmities.

I would not willingly offend you,
and I therefore rely upon the merits of my Saviour
and will never despair of your mercy.

PRAYERS IN TIMES OF

JOY AND THANKSGIVING
TROUBLE OR DIFFICULTY
TEMPTATION

KNOWING GOD

Almighty God,
because I cannot form right apprehensions of you
by the dim light of nature,
I thank you because you, in your mercy
and knowing that the happiness of man
cannot be secured without that knowledge,
have condescended to reveal
that which reason is too weak to discover.

You have directed me and all men
to search and find you as you are in Jesus Christ,
in whom dwells the fullness of your Godhead bodily.
For me to know our Lord only as a man
is to learn that I have done,
and daily do,
many things contrary to your Divine nature
and the dictates of my own reason,
which must necessarily lead me to despair.

But to behold you in Jesus Christ,
reconciling the world unto yourself:
by faith to see you, the infinite, all-glorious Being,
assuming the character of a Saviour,
a repairer of the lapses
and healer of our diseases and miseries,
penetrates and melts my soul.

It is something my heart feels and labours under,
but my tongue cannot express.
I adore you, O God,
I adore!

PRAISE FOR OUR CREATION

We must rest that we may adore and praise you,
your infinite power, wisdom and goodness,
all that is displayed in this beauteous fabric of the world,
in the noble system of all created beings.

We must praise you, too,
for our own creation, preservation,
and all the blessings that we partake of
in common with the rest of your creatures.

More particularly,
we praise you for all special or peculiar favours –
such as health; friends;
a comfortable and convenient habitation;
for any extraordinary deliverances from,
or supports under, troubles;
and for all mercies we enjoy.

DIVINE ILLUMINATION

I will praise you, my God,
for illuminating my mind,
and for enabling me to prove demonstrably
that your wisdom is as infinite as your power.

The use I am to make of these discoveries
is to praise you, and to love you, and to obey you.
Therefore I will be exceedingly careful
that my affections keep pace with knowledge,
for if I study your different perfections
as a matter of mere speculation,
that knowledge will but enhance my guilt,
and increase my future torment.

I must know that I may adore and love
and if I am now more rationally persuaded
that God is infinitely wise,
then I must learn by this knowledge,
to practise a more hearty and universal subjection to you,
and more cheerfully submit to the order of your Providence.

GOD'S BOUNDLESS GOODNESS

O God,
I stand amazed at your boundless
and inexhaustible goodness and mercy!
That you should give so much
to those who are so undeserving,
so unmindful of you,
and so regardless and unthankful for your mercies.

This is not after the manner of man, O Lord!
As the heavens are higher than the earth,
so are your thoughts higher than ours.
If we, your sinful creatures,
do a small, inconsiderable kindness for anyone,
we expect that it should never be forgotten,
and greatly resent the least shadow of ingratitude.

But how easily do we forget to praise you for your daily
        mercies,
and though we think that the want
of any one convenience or comfort is sufficient
to justify our complaints and murmurings,
even though we have innumerable blessings
at the order of your Providence,
of which we are unworthy,
yet when we do not feel the want of them
we find it very hard to preserve
an habitual sense of your goodness and a grateful temper
        of mind.

And yet your provision maintains its constant course,
and you go on after a manner worthy of God
to shower down blessings on an unthankful world.
You will have mercy because you will have mercy!
Even so, Father; for so it seems good in your sight!
Glory be to the Father! Son! and Holy Ghost!

GOD WORKS IN US

Help me, Almighty God,
not to provoke you by my unbelief
to withdraw your Spirit from me.

Help me
to call to remembrance your past mercies
when you restrained me
from a vain and sinful consummation.
And enable me not to think so unworthily of you,
as that your power or goodness is now less than it was.

May I always give God the glory of his grace.
For I am assured that I am nothing but corruption and misery,
and if ever I am restrained from anything that is good,
I will give you the praise,
for it is all owing to your undeserved grace,
if you either will or do,
according to your good pleasure.
Glory be to you, O Lord!

THE MERCIES OF GOD

Praise God, my soul,
and all that is within me bless his holy Name.
May I thankfully recognise the mercies of this day hitherto;
the assistance of your Holy Spirit in family devotion;
the disposition and ability to speak of you;
to instruct the children;
to perform all domestic duties;
the health and preservation of myself and family
from all ill accidents, terrors and dangers.

Surely the tribute of our praise
is an indispensable and pleasing duty.
May I heartily thank that Omnipotent Goodness,
that you have preserved me from all presumptuous sins,
and I will trust in and rely on Jesus Christ
for the supply of my deficiencies,
and firmly believe
that as Almighty God imputed Adam's sin to all his posterity,
so he will upon account of the just obedience
his only Son paid to the Divine laws in my nature,
accept of my sincere though otherwise imperfect obedience.
Glory be to you, O Lord!

IN ALL THINGS

Almighty God,
I think myself highly obliged
to adore and praise your unsearchable wisdom
and boundless goodness
for this dispensation of your Providence towards me.

For I clearly discern
there is more of mercy in this disappointment of my hopes
than there would have been
in permitting me to enjoy all that I had desired
because it has given me a sight of
and sense of some sins
which before I could not have imagined
and I was in the least inclined to,
including idolatry and covetousness,
and want of practical subjection to your will.

NO SHADOW OF TURNING

I would speak magnificently of you, Almighty God,
the High and Lofty One,
the Creator – who inhabits eternity.
I would speak magnificently and more worthily of you.
You are immense, infinitely perfect mind.
Holiness is your essence,
the eternal, infinite rectitude of your nature.

You are absolutely separated from all moral imperfection,
there is no contrariness or contradiction in you,
no variableness neither shadow of turning.
You are power, wisdom, justice, goodness and truth.
You are perfection of being,
who comprehends all and infinitely more than we can possibly
    conceive.

You are essential glory,
nor can your glory admit of excess or diminution
by any act of your creatures.
It is an impropriety of speech to say we glorify your Name,
for it is the exercise of your mercy and goodness upon man
that reflects your glory on these perfections.

TAKING UP THE CROSS

My God,
I thank you for the abundant reason I have
to adore, to praise and to magnify your goodness and love
in sending your Son into the world to die for sinners.

I have so much reason to praise, adore and love
that Saviour who suffered so much to redeem me!
What sentiments of gratitude should I conceive
for such boundless charity to souls!
Help me, Lord,
to gladly and cheerfully take up my cross
for him who suffered death upon the cross for me.

Enable me to praise and adore your blessèd Spirit,
who sanctifies and illumines the mind;
who co-operates with the means of grace;
who condescends to visit and assist and refresh my soul by his
     powerful influences.
Glory be to the Father, Son and Holy Spirit,
joint Authors of my salvation.

COMMIT YOUR WAY TO THE LORD

O Lord,
I thank you
because never once in my life
have I been unheard in what I feared,
when I have approached you
in a full sense of my own impotence of mind,
with humility and sincerity to implore your Divine assistance.

I set to my seal that you are true,
since I have ever found you so.
Forbid it that I should venture upon any business
without first begging your direction and assistance.
So set a check upon my mind
when I would do anything that I know to be unlawful or
    dubious,
and encourage me
with hopes of success in my lawful undertakings.

SINCERE DEVOTION

O God, I find it most difficult
to preserve a devout and serious temper of mind
in the midst of much worldly business.

Were I permitted to choose a state of life,
or positively to ask of you anything in this world,
I would humbly choose and beg
that I might be placed in such a station
wherein I might have daily bread with moderate care
and that I might have more leisure to retire from the world
without injuring those dependent upon me.

Yet I do not know
whether such a state of life would really be the best for me;
nor am I assured that if I had more leisure
I should be more zealously devoted to you
and serve you better than now.

Therefore, O Lord,
show me that it is undoubtedly best
to keep my mind in habitual submission and resignation to you,
you who are infinitely, incomprehensibly wise and good;
who cannot possibly err,
but who does certainly know what is best for your children
and how and where to fix the bounds of their habitation:
who has given to us your Word,
that all things shall work together for good
to those that love you;
may that Word support and calm my mind
in all adverse or uneasy circumstances of life.

THE YOKE OF GOD

Enable me, Lord,
to take courage
and to suffer not my mind to faint or grow weary,
knowing that you, my God,
are no hard Master,
and though it may seem best to your infinite wisdom
to determine me to such a station
as will necessarily involve me in much business
and so daily exercise my faith and patience,
yet enable me to rest in the assurance
that all things shall at least have a happy end,
if my heart be but sincerely devoted to you.

Help me, O Lord,
to make a true use of all disappointments
and calamities in this life,
in such a way
that they might unite my heart more closely with you.

BE STRONG IN THE LORD

Lord, help us all to resolve
not to be much concerned
at what is met with in this world –
however contrary to our present inclinations.

Help us to see that whatever occurs,
events are ordered by your unerring wisdom –
a wisdom that disposes of all things;
that fixes the bounds;
and determines the place of our habitation.

Help us to endure all things with patience
as we see the end of all troubles to be at hand,
for life passes most quickly.

Remind us that in a few years –
perhaps days –
we shall pass into another state very different from this,
wherein we shall always enjoy that tranquillity
that is in vain sought for in any temporal enjoyment,
nor shall we sin or sorrow more.
Help us to encourage each other, then,
as we think on eternity.

BEING A GOOD SOLDIER

O God,
help me to bear severe reflections;
unjust censures;
contemptuous words and unreasonable actions –
without perturbation;
without rendering evil for evil;
but with an equal temper cheerfully do my duty.

For when I can bear these things
and act in this manner,
it is then that I know
you have given me some degree of humility and resignation.

GOD NEVER FORGETS US

Lord, I do not,
and by your grace will not,
despair.
For even when I was almost without hope,
when I had forgotten you,
I found you had not forgotten me.
Even then you did by your Spirit,
apply the merits of the great Atonement to my soul,
by telling me that your Son died for me.

And if the God of truth,
the Almighty Saviour,
tells me that I am interested in his blood and righteousness,
shall I not believe him?
God forbid!

I do, I will believe;
and though I am the greatest of sinners,
that does not discourage me,
for all my transgressions are the sins of a finite person,
but the merits of my Lord's sufferings and righteousness are
    infinite!

God forbid that I should renounce the little Christianity I have;
nay, let me rather grow in grace
and in the knowledge of our Lord and Saviour Jesus Christ.
Amen.

PEACE WHICH PASSES
ALL UNDERSTANDING

O God,
let it be my great care
to have special regard to justice and charity;
to preserve the principles of faith inviolate;
and in all cases
to perform present duty
with the greatest exactness and integrity.

May it be, my Lord,
that whenever crosses or troubles are met without,
let all be well within,
and may the consciousness of my own innocence
be an admirable preservative against all exterior calamities!

Grant it, Lord,
that it may not be the power of any
to rob me of that peace which results from a firm trust in you,
through the merits of our blessèd Saviour,
to whom,
with you and the Sacred Spirit,
be all glory!

LIVING THE GOSPEL

Lord, why do I not take more care to practise my own rules?
For what reason or for what end do I write them down
if not that I might remember to practise them
in my life in the world?

Help me, therefore,
to keep my affections under due control
and to be careful not to offend
in speaking of persons who are absent;
for I am convinced that it is my duty so to do.
Help me to be more careful for the future
not to be guilty in this matter,
lest by sinning against the checks of the conscience,
I provoke the Holy Spirit to forsake me.

DELIVER US FROM TEMPTATION

I resolve not to be discouraged
in times of bodily weakness.
All the more will I endeavour
to keep my mind as composed as possible,
and I will pray to you, Lord,
to preserve me from temptation during these times –
and that as my day is so my strength might be.

Though you as a merciful being
never expose us or lead us into temptation
with a design to ensnare or betray our virtue,
yet oftentimes,
for reasons not always obvious,
you do permit ill men and evil angels
to afflict your servants very severely.

Help us to remember
that in James you tell us:
happy is the man that endures temptation.
With submission I would pray,
Blessèd is the man whom God by his Providence
preserves from too great or constant trials.

Amen, Lord Jesus.

TAKING UP OUR CROSS

He that sits on the throne shall feed us,
and shall lead us unto living fountains of water.
Far be from us to think that the grace of God
can be purchased with anything less precious
than the blood of Jesus.

But if it could,
who that has the lowest degree of faith
would not part with all things in this world
to obtain that love for our dear Redeemer
which we so long for and sigh after?

Here we cannot watch one hour with Jesus
without weariness;
failure of spirits;
dejection of mind;
worldly regards which damp our devotions;
and pollute the purity of our sacrifices.

And what Christian does not often feel and bewail
the weight of corrupt nature and
the many infirmities which molest us in our way to glory?
And how difficult is it to practise as we ought
that great duty of self-denial;
to take up our cross;
and follow the Captain of our salvation,
without ever repining or murmuring!

If shame or confusion could enter those blessèd mansions,
how would our souls be ashamed and confounded
at the review of our imperfect services
when we see them crowned
with such an unprofitable reward?
How shall we blush!

THE POWER OF PRAYER

You have shown me, Lord,
that philosophy and morality are not sufficient
to restrain me from those sins
that the constitution of my body
and the circumstances of my life
strongly dispose me to.

I find nature and appetite to be too hard for their precepts.
They might teach me caution
and give a check to vicious inclinations in public,
but they will never carry me
to an inward and universal purity:
for this can only be effected by the power of religion,
which will direct me to a serious application to you,
my God, in fervent prayer.

It is then that I shall feel a disengagement
from the impressions that sensual objects
are wont to make on my mind,
and in inward strength of disposition to resist them.

Therefore, I pray for that
which all good people have felt,
upon their frequent application to you in prayer, namely –
a freedom from those ill impressions that formerly subdued me;
an inward love to virtue and true goodness;
and an easiness and delight in all the parts of holiness
that are fed and cherished in me
by a seriousness in prayer.

REJOICE IN THE LORD

It is in this that we may rejoice:
that we are in the hand of a God who never did
and who never can –
exert his power in any act of injustice, oppression or cruelty,
in the power of that Superior Wisdom
which disposes all events,
and has promised that all things
shall work together for good,
for the spiritual and eternal good of those that love him.

We may rejoice in hope
that Almighty Goodness will not suffer us
to be tempted above that we are able,
but will with the temptation
make a way to escape that we may be able to bear it.

In a word,
we may and we ought to rejoice
that God has assured us that he will never leave us nor
forsake us.
But if we continue to be faithful to him,
he will take care to conduct us safely
through all the changes and chances of this mortal life
to those blessèd regions of joy and immortality
where sin and sorrow can never enter.

STANDING IN GOD'S STRENGTH

I thank you, O God,
for your Holy Spirit,
who illuminates my mind
that I may have a clearer perception of you and of
spiritual things,
for this strengthens my soul and raises my affections.

Help me to always beware
and to keep a stronger guard upon myself,
lest by unfaithfulness to your good Spirit,
I provoke you to withdraw your influences
and so leave me in a state of uncomfortable darkness.

Deliver me from that inequality of temper
which comes through my own inadvertence,
and a presumption of my own strength
which would render me careless of improving the graces of life
and unmindful of the many temptations
to which I am hourly exposed, and which,
by reason of their smallness,
I am apt to despise,
when in truth,
these lesser but numerous temptations
are the greater trials of our virtue.

THE WAY TO THE FATHER

O my God,
if it will please you indeed to bless me,
and deliver me from temptations,
if you will vouchsafe to give me food to eat
and raiment to put on,
without debt;
without this extreme distress;
then I will offer up my self absolutely,
entirely to Jesus Christ,
the Incarnate God,
the only Saviour of the world!

To be instructed by his Spirit,
strengthened and directed by him,
to amend in each particular failing,
since there is no name under heaven given unto men,
whereby they may be saved, but that of the Lord Jesus!

And no man can come unto the Father but by him!
He is our Way, our Truth, our Life!

GOD'S GOOD GOVERNMENT

Very heartily and earnestly do I pray to you, O God,
for strength to govern and regulate my passions.
It is not in us who walk to direct our own steps,
therefore I humbly implore you
to steer my soul by your Holy Spirit,
through all the intricate scenes of human life.

I pray too that I might depend not
on my own strength or wisdom,
believing that you will guide me by your counsel
and at last conduct me to your glory.

MEDITATIONS ON

THE NATURE OF GOD
THE BLESSINGS OF GOD
THE LORD'S DAY

THE TRANSCENDENCE OF GOD

Almighty God,
I long for a just sense of you
as Father, Son and Holy Spirit.

After so many years of inquiry,
so long reading and so much thinking,
your boundless essence appears more inexplicable,
the perfection of your glory more bright and inaccessible.
Your sublimity transcends all thought;
words cannot express what is so far above their nature;
therefore the simplest and plainest are the best.

I cannot do you the justice that I would.
I cannot, by the utmost force and energy of all my powers,
attain to the proper knowledge of your essence,
your essential glory,
wherein all perfections concentre.

Yet enable me
to discover the emanations of that glory;
the manifestations it has made or makes of itself,
in the exercise of your Divine perfections,
in the creation of the world,
the redemption of our human nature
and the government of the world,
particularly in respect to mankind.

THE GLORY OF GOD

There are no words in ours,
nor in all the languages on earth
whereby to express infinity –
but when we consider God's nature – his Being –
this includes infinity.

Whatever glory we ascribe to him
such as power, wisdom,
justice, goodness,
truth and holiness,
are not in him
distinct powers or acquired virtues
superadded to his essence,
they are his very essence itself!

Therefore, though we often call him a wise,
a powerful, a holy, and a just God –
yet if we would speak properly we should say,
He is Wisdom! Power!
Justice! Goodness! and Truth!
For God is One!

The infinity of God, therefore,
tells us that his Being –
His essential perfection –
is immense!
It is without bounds or limits!
His power inexhaustible!
His knowledge, wisdom and goodness
are absolutely perfect.

GOD IS TRUTH

I worship you
when I see
that the direction of your infinite wisdom,
justice and goodness
are so immutably bent towards or fixed on truth –
that it is impossible for you to err or swerve the least
from the most perfect truth and purity in your actions.

Instead you always purpose what is certainly and
absolutely best!
Nor are you capable of fraud or falsehood,
which are diametrically opposite to your nature!
And as it is impossible for you to be deceived,
so it is impossible for you ever to deceive!

GOD IS HOLY

O Lord,
it is certain that your holiness
is not a distinct perfection in your most blessèd being,
but rather it is the supreme glory of your other attributes!

It is the glory of your power
that you are perfectly holy!
There is no mixture of weakness in you;
no capacity of being employed in any act of injustice,
oppression or cruelty!

Your knowledge and wisdom too, are pure,
in that they are absolutely perfect!
They are unstained by ignorance and error;
nor can they possibly be applied to any end or use,
but what is infinitely best!

It is the glory of your goodness –
to be pure!
It is the glory of your truth –
to be eternal! Simple! Undisguised!
Infinitely incapable of being polluted by guile and falsehood!
You who created all things –
can never change for the better,
so neither can you change for the worse!

TRUE KNOWLEDGE OF GOD

This is eternal life – to know you,
the only true God,
and Jesus Christ whom you have sent.

But what is it to know God?
What is that knowledge of God on which eternal life depends?
For even from the primordials of the universe
do we collect that there is one supreme,
eternal, consequently self-existent Being,
who gave being to all things.

Creation, though, demonstrates your omnipotence –
which includes your wisdom,
justice, truth, purity and goodness.
For all these are perfections
and were you deficient in one,
you would not be omnipotent.

But you are a Spirit unbodied;
undetermined;
immense;
filling heaven and earth;
most pure and uncompounded;
and absolutely separated and free
from whatever pollution a Spirit is capable of being defiled with.

You are immutable;
incapable of change or alteration for the better or worse.
perfectly free;
knowing no superior;
no equal that may impel, allure or persuade you;
but acting always spontaneously
according to the counsel of your own will.

I do not despise nor neglect the light of reason,
nor that knowledge of you which by her conduct
may be collected from this goodly system of created beings.

But all this is to know you only reasonably,
as Creator, Preserver and Governor of the universe;
and this is not that knowledge that leads us to eternal life –
this speculative knowledge
is not the knowledge I want and wish for.

I want to know you in my heart and will and affections,
not merely as the Author of my being
but as Healer and Repairer of our broken human nature.
Thus let me ever know you, O God!

THE LOVE THAT OVERWHELMS US

Lord,
who can think, much less speak,
on the vast subject of the Godhead?
Your greatness,
your dignity astonishes us!
The purity of your nature
and your redeeming love,
confounds and overpowers us!

At the perception of your glory,
our feeble powers are suspended,
and nature faints before the God of nature.
I dare not say I love you,
only that I have chosen you
for my own happiness,
my all, my only good;
in a word – for my God.

That you are everywhere present,
and we always present to you is certain,
but that we should always be able to realise
your presence is quite another thing.

You are so infinitely blessèd,
so absolutely lovely,
that every perception of you,
every approach to your supreme glory and blessèdness,
imparts such a vital joy and gladness to my mind,
as banishes all pain and sense of misery,
and were eternity added to this happiness,
it would be heaven.

DIVINE MEDITATION

God is a boundless, inexhaustible subject for thought,
and though we should spend an eternity in contemplation
of any one of his Divine perfections,
we could never attain to an adequate conception thereof.

I say this not to discourage,
but to inspire your soul with vigour and to show you
that if the mind be but effectually touched with the love of God,
it is almost impossible that any of that sacred time
should lie dead upon our hands,
or that such a soul should be idle,
or not fully employed
which has a strong and clear perception of that most
blessèd Spirit.

But Oh – what purity,
what separation from the world and all material objects,
what intenseness of thought,
and actual response to the presence of the great and holy God,
is necessary when we apply ourselves
to the contemplation of his most glorious perfections!

GOD'S FAVOUR IN CHRIST

The noblest wine,
the most generous cordial,
does not so much exhilarate and cheer the spirit
as the least perception of your favour through Jesus Christ
does refresh and gladden the soul.

And all the more,
when the soul is ready to faint
under the weight of its corrupt nature,
and when we have been in an unsuccessful pursuit of
happiness –
in the enjoyment of what the world calls good.

It is in these lucid intervals,
when the soul by contemplation holds you in view,
that we say with your Apostle:
'Master, it is good for us to be here!'

Supreme Eternal Being!
Fountain of life and happiness!
Vouchsafe to be for ever present
to the inward sense of my mind;
and as I offer you my heart
take possession by your Holy Spirit.

GOD'S LAW

Glory be to you, O Lord,
for your infinite wisdom in giving to rational free agents,
a Law suitable to their natures,
and tending to their happiness!

The whole substance matter of the Law of reason
is briefly summed up in these two comprehensive duties –
the love of God and the love of man,
and upon these two,
hang all the Law and the Prophets.

THE PATIENCE OF GOD

How inconceivable
and how incomprehensibly great
is your goodness and patience towards sinful man!

How many sins does one sinner commit
in the short compass of one day
against your most glorious majesty,
either in thought, word, or deed?
Then how innumerable are the sins of the whole world!

Yet you do not take vengeance
though you could in a moment
consume them.
My God,
you are strong and patient
though you are provoked every day.

The works of your creation
and the redemption of the world by Jesus Christ
demonstrate your omnipotence,
yet your power over yourself
which appears by your sustaining the affronts,
contempt and insults of your rebellious creatures
appear to me as clearer proofs
of your merciful and powerful nature.

GOD'S UNIVERSAL DOMINION

Your dominion, O Lord,
is a universal dominion,
and your Kingdom rules over all.
Your authority is indisputable
and has been acknowledged by all
that have acknowledged your existence.

As by your physical power
you have an ability to act as you please,
so by your moral power
you have an undoubted right to do whatsoever pleases you.
Is it not lawful for you to do what you will with your own?
Glory be to you, O Lord!

Your dominion, O God,
is founded on the superlative excellence of your nature.
As none but God could possibly create
this universal system of beings,
so none but he could have taught
and deservedly challenged the government of it,
he being the supreme and most excellent of Beings.

KING OVER ALL

I thank you, O God,
for the relief and satisfaction of mind
that come with the firm assurance
that you do govern the world;
for the patience and resignation to your providence
that are afforded as I reflect
that even the tumultuous and irregular actions of sinful men are
nevertheless under your direction,
you who are wise,
good and omnipotent,
and who has promised
to make all things work together for good
to them that love you.

WE OUGHT ALWAYS TO PRAY

Glory be to you, O Lord.
Though through infirmities I can rarely
exert the powers of the soul and
vigorously attend on your service –
yet because my heart is sincere
I will hope for acceptance.

Fill me with your love
that I may overcome the impediments of
little time,
a great deal of weakness,
and much business.

Purify my mind from all worldly regards,
that I might cease from desiring any applause from man,
whose breath is in his nostrils
and who is of no account.
Help me to apply myself vigorously to seeking you,
but without power I cannot.
The mind of man is naturally so corrupted,
and all the powers thereof so weakened,
that we cannot possibly aspire vigorously towards God,
or have any clear perception of spiritual things,
without your assistance.

Because your grace is worth waiting for,
I will not be discouraged;
and I will remember the words of my Saviour,
'That men ought always to pray,
and not to faint.'

THE MERCY OF GOD

Glory be to you, O Lord,
for though we were so corrupt and impure by nature;
the children of wrath and in a state of damnation;
eternally separated from him who is our life;
yet through your infinite goodness,
you would not suffer the whole race of mankind
to be ruined and destroyed by the fraud and subtilty of Satan.

You delighted that your mercy should triumph over your justice,
for though you provided no remedy for the fallen angels,
you laid help upon One that is mighty,
that is able and willing to save to the uttermost
all such as shall come unto God through him.

Our Saviour is that Seed of the woman,
that was promised should bruise the head of the serpent;
break the power of the devil;
and bring mankind again into a salvable condition.
You have renewed your covenant with us,
not on the former condition of perfect obedience,
but on condition of faith in Christ Jesus,
and a sincere though imperfect obedience to the laws of God.

THE GOOD SHEPHERD

Lord,
be with me in those times of deep adversity,
when my mind is affected
and I am disposed to anxious, doubtful
and unbelieving thoughts.

Even if I make no direct murmurings,
no repinings at the prosperity of others,
no harsh reflections on Providence,
I know this does not mean
that I am not in the power of the world,
and innocent of immoderate anxious care.

Help me always,
to have a constant acknowledgement
of your justice and goodness;
that you punish less than our iniquities deserve;
and that in the midst of judgement
you always remember mercy.

Deliver me
from thinking severely or unjustly of others;
from being too much dejected;
or disposed to peevishness, covetousness,
or negligence in affairs;
and from working too much or too little.

Forgive me,
when through presumption or despondency,
I wholly omit to implore your divine blessing and assistance
in honest prospects and endeavours;
or when I am too solicitous and earnest in prayer
for external blessings.

Help me not to think so much on my circumstances
that my privacy is invaded,
and my rest disturbed.

Let no small access of trouble
have the power to ruffle my temper,
or to indispose or distract my mind –
in addresses to heaven,
in reading,
in meditation,
or in any other spiritual exercise.

Help me
to observe what you have said by your Apostle,
that we should be careful – anxious for nothing.
Moreover we should remember
that you rank cares of this life
as mortal damning sins.

GOD IS FAITHFUL

Even though we are born to trouble
I thank you, my God,
that I believe there would hardly be anyone found
upon the whole earth compared to me,
who has had in their lives,
more mercies than afflictions
and much more pleasure than pain.

Though for many years I have suffered much pain
and great bodily infirmities,
yet I have likewise enjoyed great intervals of rest and ease.
But all those sufferings of mine have,
by your blessing,
been of excellent use,
and proved the most proper means of reclaiming me
from a vain and sinful life.
Inasmuch that I cannot say
I would have been better without this affliction,
this disease, this loss, want, contempt or reproach.

In fact, all my sufferings –
by the admirable management of your omnipotent goodness –
have concurred to promote my spiritual and eternal good.
If I have not reaped that advantage by my sufferings
which I might have done,
it will be merely owing
to the perverseness of my own will;
my frequent lapses into present things;
and my unfaithfulness to your good Spirit.

I give you glory, O Lord,
because notwithstanding all my prevarications
and all the stupid opposition I have made,
you have never totally abandoned me.

GOD IS ALL IN ALL

O God,
You are all in all
and those whom you bless
shall be blessed indeed.
Therefore I would entirely resign myself
and all my fortunes to Almighty God.
And may that Infinite Being,
whose we are
and whom I hope we endeavour to serve and love,
accept and bless us.

THE GIFT OF THE SPIRIT

Since you were pleased to send your Holy Spirit
in an extraordinary manner upon the apostles,
so that they were enabled to propagate
the Christian faith,
and to preach the Gospel of Jesus Christ
and the glad tidings of salvation to the sons of men,
may the first thing I do this morning with great humility
be to implore the Divine Majesty
that he would for the sake of this same Jesus
whom they preached
to grant me his Holy Spirit
in such a measure as is necessary
for my believing and obeying that blessèd Gospel
that I may be a partaker of those heavenly gifts
which through Christ are bestowed on true believers.

GOD IS EVERYTHING

Lord, I am nothing!
I have nothing!
I can do nothing!

I am nothing in a moral sense.
I have no power to walk conformably to your laws,
by reason of my pride and concupiscence.
I have nothing that I can properly call my own but sin
    and misery,
no moral or intellectual goodness
but what is given from above.

GOD'S ENDOWMENT

I thank you, my God,
because I know that religion does not mean
melancholy and moroseness,
which tends only to destroy the comforts of our
environment.

But I have learned
that all things in the world where religion is absent,
cannot possibly make men happy
or easy to themselves or others.

I have learnt too,
that whatever I enjoy of the good things of this life
is attained with so much vanity and vexation of spirit,
that my happiness even in this world,
depends entirely on your favour.
When I am peevish and morose,
it is not because of religion,
but my want of it.

Help me, my God,
not to be discouraged by my own failures,
nor too spend too much time in thinking on them,
remembering that perfection is your endowment
and that sincerity is mine.
Help me with firm faith to rely on your merits,
joined with my sincere endeavour to obey your whole will.

THE DAY OF THE LORD

Almighty God –
we are yours
and it is to you
that we are indebted for all the time we enjoy.

It has pleased you to set apart a seventh part thereof
to your more immediate service –
thereby indulging us rest and leisure after six days' labour
to attend upon your public ordinances.
This you have done that we may be somewhat refreshed
by the contemplation of yourself in the wondrous works
of your creation and providence.

It is therefore our duty,
to remember this most happy day before it comes
so that we may prevent as much as possibly we can,
being encumbered or divested on that day,
by any unnecessary business,
impertinent visits,
or whatever else may rob us
of any of those sacred moments
which ought to be all devoted to you,
for it is a kind of sacrilege to alienate them from your service.

GOD'S DAY OF REST

In six days you made heaven and earth,
the sea and all that in them is,
and on the seventh day you rested.
Wherefore you blessed the seventh day and
hallowed it.
Therefore,
in imitation of you, the great Creator,
help us also to rest,
rest from all our worldly business.

PUBLIC WORSHIP

Since our blessèd Saviour –
by his resurrection on the first day of the week;
by his sending the Holy Ghost on that day;
by his own example;
and by his Spirit in the apostles and primitive church,
has changed the observation of the seventh
to the first day of the week,
the business of the day is enlarged.

And we must now not only bless God
for all his works of creation and providence,
but we must humbly offer to God the Father, Son and
Holy Ghost,
our highest prayers
for the redemption of the world by the Holy Jesus.

And this we must do publicly in the assembly of the saints,
for the more public our devotions are on that day,
provided they are hearty and sincere,
the more do we honour God
because we thereby excite others to worship him also,
and we show unto the world
that we are not ashamed of professing ourselves
the disciples of a crucified Jesus.

IN THE SPIRIT

Lord, I implore your divine assistance,
that you might enable me
to spend every moment of that most precious time –
the day that you have given to us –
as becomes those who have devoted themselves to you.

I beg of you, my God,
that you might
turn my mind from all vain and worldly thoughts;
compose and regulate my affections;
and elevate my soul to such a devout and holy temper,
that I might know by experience what it is
to be in the Spirit on the Lord's Day.
May I also know by experience, my God,
that religion is more than a vain fancy or illusion.

GOD'S BLESSING OF REST

Lord,
I would remember the Sabbath Day that I might keep it holy,
as I remember that you too keep holy the Sabbath Day,
blessèd God!

Why should we even need your memento
to put us in mind of such inestimable blessing?
To labour six days indeed is hard,
so why do we stand in need of a command
to make us cheerfully undergo so difficult a task?

It is a most pleasing and desirable thing
that after having spent six days in the business of this life,
you command us to rest.
And we should be so grateful
that we know that we cannot
sufficiently bless and praise our God
for giving us leave to enjoy a Sabbath;
for permitting us to refresh our souls,
by a view of that rest and glory,
which he has prepared for those that love him.

Let us all agree to devote the day to God
in obedience to God's command,
or under the notion of a free-will offering,
if God will be pleased with my strict observation of the day,
it is sufficient for me,
it is all I ask,
and whatever others may think or do,
I account this the most blessèd and happy day of the week.

Enable us to spend more time and care
in adorning our minds with such virtues
as become those who profess godliness,
so that we will not be so solicitous
about these perishing bodies
to have them appear well-dressed,
which often-times proves a snare
not only to ourselves but to others also.

BE HOLY

Almighty God,
it is needless to inform us
how a great part of this your day must be employed,
since we already know that it is our duty
to attend upon the public worship of God,
and that we ought to behave ourselves
with great gravity and reverence
when we come into your holy temple.

When we are in your presence,
and under the more immediate inspection of such a great
God, remind us
that when we hold communion with the saints,
we are with all the celestial hierarchy;
with angels and archangels;
and with all the company of the heavenly host.

Together we join in worshipping,
in praising and adoring our great Creator,
our blessèd Redeemer and that Holy Spirit
by whom we are sealed unto the day of redemption.

I am very sure, Lord,
that if we did but actually dwell
on the awful presence we are then in,
and did but seriously attend to the business we come about,
it would restrain our thoughts and eyes from wandering;
nor should we find leisure to observe any about us;
or desire to be taken notice of ourselves;
much less should we stand upon ceremony and compliment
which are at best but trifles in any place,
but are scandalous and abominable in your house.

THE CAPTAIN OF OUR SALVATION

We bless you, Lord, that you steer our souls
innocently through this tempestuous world.
You calm and support us,
under all the calamities of human life.
Peace was the legacy of our dying Lord,
and as the world cannot give it,
so neither can it take it away.

Though the corruption of our natures
too often gives advantage to our spiritual enemy
to disturb and discompose our minds,
may it be that those persons who are truly devoted to God,
have habitually such an inward peace,
and tranquillity of soul,
as none eye can possibly can conceive or enjoy,
especially on the Sabbath, that blessèd day of God,
which you have in your abundant, infinite goodness,
given to the sons of men,
as a type and foretaste of that eternal rest
that you have promised with yourself in glory.

And if we have reason to bless the Divine goodness,
for feeding and clothing us,
for so liberally indulging us so many mercies
in our passage through this world,
help us to see that we have much more reason
to praise, to magnify, and to adore
your boundless love and goodness to mankind
in permitting us to enjoy such an inestimable blessing
as a Sabbath,
after six days' labour.

Let us then rejoice when your day approaches
and in our morning retirement
endeavour to prepare our minds
for the solemn, happy employment of it.

And with all my heart and soul and mind and strength
I adore and praise you,
O eternal and ever-blessèd God,
for giving me a dispensation
from all worldly business for this day
and, since the weakness and corruption
of human nature requires it,
for commanding us to keep holy the Sabbath day.

Therefore with angels and archangels
we praise and magnify you,
O God the Father, Son and Holy Ghost
to whom be glory and praise for ever and ever.
Amen.

Notes And Sources

Page *Prayer Titles*

5. True friendship: Untitled Susanna mss
6. True riches: Wesley Banner p285
7. Seize the opportunity: Wesley Banner p366
8. Redeem the time: Susanna Letters to Samuel Wesley May 22nd 1709
9. The Name of the Lord: Susanna mss D2/6 p82-3
10. A living sacrifice: Untitled Susanna mss
11. Living in God's presence: Untitled Susanna mss
12. Obedience is better than sacrifice: Untitled Susanna mss
13. Trust in the Lord: Untitled Susanna mss
14. Practising the presence of God: Untitled Susanna mss
15. Help me to know myself: Untitled Susanna mss
16. Purify my mind: Untitled Susanna mss
17. True contentment: Untitled Susanna mss
18. A good conscience: Wesley Banner p284
19. Strong in the Lord: Wesley Banner p285
20. Family responsibilities: Wesley Banner p286-7
21. Love not the world: Susanna mss D2/2 p12
22. The virtue of obedience: Susanna mss D2/2 p17
23. The most powerful Teacher: Susanna mss D2/2 p20
24. Only God can satisfy: Untitled Susanna mss
25. Saved by grace: Untitled Susanna mss
26. Knowing God: Untitled Susanna mss
27. Man's first duty: Untitled Susanna mss
28. God answers prayer: Untitled Susanna mss
29. Continued
30. Continued
31. Lord, I love you: Susanna mss D2/3 p3
32. Growing toward God's likeness: Untitled Susanna mss
33. For my children: Susanna mss D2/6 p93-4
34. Pure service: Susanna mss D2/6 p128
35. True devotion: Untitled Susanna mss
36. Lord of Creation: Untitled Susanna mss
37. Watch and pray: Untitled Susanna mss
38. Resting and trusting: Untitled Susanna mss
39. The Lord's Supper: Wesley Banner p404
40. God's mercy: Wesley Banner p404
41. Lord of all: Susanna Letters May 22nd 1706
42. Cleanse me, O Lord: Untitled Susanna mss

43. Abundant cleansing: Untitled Susanna mss
44. Your grace makes me what I am: Untitled Susanna mss
47. Knowing God: Untitled Susanna mss
48. Praise for our creation: Susanna mss D2/6 p85
49. Divine illumination: Susanna mss D2/6 p130
50. God's boundless goodness: Untitled Susanna mss
51. God works in us: Untitled Susanna mss
52. The mercies of God: Untitled Susanna mss
53. In all things: Untitled Susanna mss
54. No shadow of turning: Untitled Susanna mss
55. Taking up the cross: Untitled Susanna mss
56. Commit your way to the Lord: Untitled Susanna mss
57. Sincere devotion: Untitled Susanna mss
58. The yoke of God: Untitled Susanna mss
59. Be strong in the Lord: Wesley Banner p284
60. Being a good soldier: Susanna mss D2/2 p10
61. God never forgets us: Susanna Letters to Charles Wesley
        October 2nd 1740
62. Peace which passes all understanding: Untitled Susanna mss
63. Living the Gospel: Wesley Banner p366
64. Deliver us from temptation: Susanna mss D2/4 p21
65. Taking up our cross: Clarke p312
66. The power of prayer: Susanna mss D2/2 p18
67. Rejoice in the Lord: Susanna Letters to John Wesley June 1735
68. Standing in God's strength: Untitled Susanna mss
69. The way to the Father: Susanna mss D2/3 p22ff
70. God's good government: Susanna mss D2/3 p24
73. The transcendence of God: Untitled Susanna mss
74. The glory of God: Susanna mss D2/4 p22
75. God is truth: Susanna mss D2/4 p40
76. God is holy: Susanna mss D2/4 p42
77. True knowledge of God: Susanna mss D2/2 p7
78. Continued
79. The love that overwhelms us: Susanna mss D2/2 p8
80. Divine meditation: Susanna mss D2/6 p97
81. God's favour in Christ: Susanna mss D2/6 p99
82. God's Law: Untitled Susanna mss
83. The patience of God: Untitled Susanna mss
84. God's universal dominion: Untitled Susanna mss
85. King over all: Untitled Susanna mss
86. We ought always to pray: Wesley Banner p404
87. The mercy of God: Clarke p291

88. The Good Shepherd: Susanna mss D2/2 p13ff
89. Continued
90. God is faithful: Susanna mss D2/2 p21
91. God is all in all: Susanna Letters May 22nd 1706
92. The gift of the Spirit: Untitled Susanna mss
93. God is everything: Untitled Susanna mss
94. God's endowment: Untitled Susanna mss
95. The Day of the Lord: Susanna mss D2/6 p83-4
96. God's day of rest: Susanna mss D2/6 p84
97. Public worship: Susanna mss D2/6 p85
98. In the Spirit: Susanna mss D2/6 p86
99. God's blessing of rest: Susanna mss D2/3 p2-3
100. Be holy: Susanna mss D2/6 p94-5
101. The Captain of our salvation: Susanna mss D2/6 p90
102. Continued

Notes on the Sources

The Wesley Banner
July-December 1852: A series of anonymous articles that appeared in this short-lived periodical, entitled 'Journal of Mrs Susanna Wesley'. The bulk of the entries are verbatim transcripts of selections from the *Manuscripts of Susanna Wesley*, which are now held in the collections of the library of Wesley College, Bristol, England.

Clarke
Adam Clarke, *Memoirs of the Wesley Family* (London, 1823).

The Susanna Manuscripts
The holdings of Wesley College include a significant amount of Wesley family material. The selections used in this volume that come directly from the manuscripts come from these and were transcribed directly by the editor of this volume.
The manuscripts include:
    'Meditations and Reflections by Mrs Susanna Wesley' (Manuscript D2/2).
    A *Notebook* containing 192 pages of meditational entries numbered from the front, and a further 19 pages of entries numbered from the rear of the *Notebook*. Susanna has dated the title page with the year 1709 (Manuscript D2/3).

There is also a third *Manuscript,* which contains three long letters written by Susanna to her son Samuel and daughter Susanna.

There are 30 further pages of her *Devotional Journal* at the rear of the *Notebook* (D2/6).

SUBJECT INDEX

Angels   100
Assurance   6, 20, 28, 58, 61
Blessing, God's   12, 24, 28, 36, 50, 51, 65, 69, 88, 90, 91, 93, 94
Business   18, 19, 35, 56, 57, 58, 86, 95, 96
Children   20, 33, 52
Christian living   14, 15, 16, 17, 18, 19, 20, 21, 22, 23, 24, 25, 26, 27,
                       28, 31, 42, 47, 57, 58, 63, 66, 80, 98
Church, the   97, 100
Cleansing   40, 42, 43
Clothing   12, 69
Commitment   35, 37, 41
Confession   41
Creation   (See Nature of God)
Death   6
Dedication   8, 10, 24, 34, 36
Devotion   5, 6, 7, 8, 9, 11, 12, 13, 14, 15, 16, 17, 18, 21, 22, 23,
                       24, 26, 27, 28, 31, 42, 44, 57, 58, 80, 98
Difficulties   13, 18, 38, 48, 53, 57, 58, 59, 60, 61, 62, 88, 90, 101
Disappointments   53, 58
Doubt   61, 88
Faith   61
Food   12, 57, 69
Forgiveness   40, 65, 83, 87
Friends   5, 48
Gifts, God's   57
God's Nature   11, 27, 34, 36, 47, 49, 54, 73, 74, 75, 76, 77, 80, 82,
                       83, 84
Growth in grace   32
Guidance   67, 70, 85, 101
Happiness   17, 94
Health   48, 52
Heaven   67, 101
Holy Spirit, the   16, 23, 51, 55, 63, 68, 69, 81, 92, 97, 98
Illness   12, 34, 44, 90
Joy   9, 10, 12, 13, 41, 44, 47, 48, 49, 50, 51, 52, 53, 54,
                       55, 56, 67, 81, 95, 97, 100
Lord's Day, the   95, 96, 97, 98, 99, 101
Lord's Supper   39
Meditation   80
Mercy   40, 50, 52, 87

Nature of God	11, 27, 34, 36, 47, 54, 73, 74, 75, 76, 77, 80, 82, 83, 84
Obedience	22, 31, 52, 94
Patience	22, 38, 59
Peace, for	13, 17, 57, 59, 62, 85, 88, 94
Persecution	60
Praise	9, 10, 12, 13, 41, 44, 46, 47, 48, 49, 50, 51, 52, 53, 54, 55, 67, 81, 95, 97, 100,
Prayer	7, 8, 9, 14, 28, 31, 33, 35, 39, 41, 52, 56, 64, 66, 70, 86, 88, 97, 100, 101
Preachers	34, 92
Providence	36, 41, 49, 50, 53, 59, 67, 84, 85, 88, 90
Refuge	67
Repentance	38, 39, 40, 41, 42, 43, 44
Rest	95, 96, 99
Sabbath, the	95, 96, 97, 98, 99, 100, 101
Salvation	49, 55, 65, 87
Security	67
Sickness	12, 35, 44, 90
Spiritual gifts	57
Spiritual warfare	31, 60, 63, 64, 65, 66, 67, 68, 69, 70, 81, 101
Strength	19, 23, 52, 65, 66, 68, 86, 94
Temptation	11, 31, 60, 63, 64, 65, 66, 67, 68, 69, 70, 81, 101
Troubles	13, 18, 38, 48, 53, 57, 58, 59, 60, 61, 62, 88, 90, 101
Trust	5, 16, 23, 24, 33, 38, 62, 67, 85, 88, 91, 101
Worries	6, 20, 61, 64, 88